Praye
A Black Man's
Soul...

With Introduction's & Scripture Quotation

By Maurice A. Petty

INTRODUCTION

Prayers for the World

Ω

Thank you for taking the time to read this book that the Lord prompted me to write while I was in the beginning stages of a major transition in my life. Some of you may have misunderstood the title of this piece of literature "Prayer's From a Black Man's Soul." You're not the only ones who may have felt that this prayer book was only written for Black Men. I'm here to tell you that this book is for anyone and everyone no matter your race, culture, or national heritage. Our Heavenly Father does not show partiality; however, He created our differences in ministry for a reason. I prayed each and every prayer in this book for all of us. Prayer's from my soul for the world. As you read these introductions to prayer's, scripture quotations, and word definitions, please keep in mind that they were all inspired by the Holy Spirit for the sharing of my personal stories, testimonies, life lessons, experience, and passion for my Lord and Savior Jesus Christ.

Anyone can relate to these prayers as they're not biased, and they're all based on morals, values, principles and ethics. They are based on truth, justice, love, unity, peace, respect, compassion and service in our lives. They are based on equality and they are all current and up to date with world matters, society, community, and household.

I was once a troubled teen, youth, and adult. I've dealt with many struggles and overcome many challenges and obstacles because of my prayers. My life has been saved, my sanity restored, the blessings received, and the grace to continue on to win the race. The power of prayer was really instilled in me when I was 14 years old while in juvenile hall. I would go to Bible studies and Church on Sundays. One pastor said something to me and the other kids in juvenile hall that always stayed close to heart. He said; pray for wisdom, knowledge, and understanding. Simple as that! I didn't understand what it all meant at the time, but I liked the idea because when I later started reading about the wisdom of David in the books of Proverbs and Psalms, I decided that's what I wanted more than anything. I learned that wisdom, knowledge and understanding gives life to all that we are as a people and believers in Christ. With wisdom, knowledge, and understanding comes character, strength, hope, success, and most importantly the faith to do all things through Christ who strengthens us.

The reason why I wrote this prayer book is because I've grown to learn that many of us don't really know how to pray. The Lord's Prayer mentions all that we need to pray for because after all, the Father knows all of our needs. However, sometimes we need to be a little more specific with our prayers. We have so many individual wants and needs, not to mention hardships, discouragement, and loss of our loved ones, lack of faith, understanding, and patience. Many of us are angry, bitter, hurt, and maybe even lost in the maze of life. We live in a big world so we often find ourselves in a world of trouble mentally, physically, emotionally and spiritually. So I wrote this book based on my experiences and the experiences of others I've encountered. It's the greatest feeling in the world to pray specific prayers, and experience the answer to that specific prayer. Even if the answer was NO...It's still an answer.

This is not the type of book that you read one chapter at a time. It's a prayer book, and its tailor made to meet most, if not all your prayer needs. The foundation of this prayer book was built on Bible Study & Bible knowledge, which means that each and every prayer is based on as well as backed up by Scripture.

In the table of contents you will find 100 prayers, along with a personal introduction, testimony, and message from the Word for each accompanying prayer. These introductions were written in order to give you more clarity and insight as to the significance of each prayer, and what you can hope for or expect, as we wait patiently for the Lord to answer our prayers.

Prayer's From a Black Man's Soul has many prayer topics that I hope and pray you take advantage of. As you pray, you must pray as if God has already answered your prayers. Our prayers might not be answered right away, but they're always on time. Let your love back up each and every prayer you pray. What are prayers without love to back them up? This is the perfect time to exercise your faith and patience. I would suggest that you keep yourself a personal journal as you pray and keep track of your answers, insights, and daily walk in faith. Please read the Scriptures that go along with each prayer because there's even more power in prayer when you have the living word of God to back you up. Keep this prayer book with you in your car, and wherever you go. The point I'm making is that these days we all need to stay "prayed up."

The Key to Words in the back of this prayer book is very valuable to understanding the words and terminologies we will be praying from Scripture. Many times we get frustrated because we don't understand some of the words or terms in the Bible. We just keep reading without really understand the words within the "Word" (The Bible). These words and their meanings are very significant to our faith as we fully understand in our minds and our hearts the words we are praying into existence.

Anyone can read Prayer's From a Black Man's Soul and meditate on them. Please feel free to share this book and purchase it for the people you love and care about as a year round gift that lasts a lifetime. The Holy Spirit has really guided me through this journey of writing my first book. I had to stay in constant prayer to make sure I had the right motives in leading others to a deeper understanding and relationship with God and Christ. I also had to put into practice all of the principles that I'm sharing with you. A lot of soul searching was involved in these prayers from my soul. There is such a thing as having a purpose in life. Prayers of faith and the Holy Spirit is what leads us to the discovery of our purposes in life.

As I travel through various communities and Churches sharing these prayers with you, I pray that we embrace the power of prayer together, and that you use the tools and ideas shared in this book to begin to master your prayer life. The proceeds from this book will be used to further missionary work in the distribution of more books in various jails, prisons, homeless shelters. Not to mention the spreading of the Word through each prayer in this book to various churches across the world. God can do so much more with our own personal stories and testimonies. He can do so much more with our talents, gifts and abilities. He will use us if we let Him. He can use our struggles and pain, trials and errors, to teach each other and bring healing in our lives as we read the stories of those who have been through the fire. I ask that you pray for this ministry so God can help us to reach out to those who really need these prayers. If the valuable principles, ideas, and prayers have touched you in a special way and you would like to partner in the furtherance of this material and future material, please send your requests at the email address provided below.

I am blessed by the prayers I've written in this book, and I pray that God may continue to bless you as He has blessed me.

God Bless You,

Maurice A. Petty *"Prayers from a Black Man's Soul"*

PrayersfromaBlackMansSoul@yahoo.com

Contents

1. Prayer to Mentor (Mt 4:18-19)
2. Prayer for Inspiration (Lk 12:2)
3. Prayer for My Talents, Gifts, & Abilities (Mt 25:14-29)
4. Prayer for Peace (Jn 14:27)
5. Prayer to Be of service (Ps 110:3, Jn 13:14, Lk 22:19, Ja 2:20)
6. Prayer for Our Designers, Builders, & Body of The Church (Ex 36:1)
7. Prayer for My Enemies (Rom 12:11-21, Lk 6:27)
8. Prayer for the Writer (Rev 1:19, 2Cor 3:2-3)
9. Prayer for Our Lawyers (Lk 11:16)
10. Prayer for the Judges (Rom 13:4-5, Duet 1:16-18)
11. Prayer for Gangs & Gang Members (Is 11:6-9)
12. Prayer to Strengthen My Character (Rom 5:3-4, Ph 2:22, Ja 1:12)
13. Prayer for the Young Man (Ecc 9:10, Ja 2:20-21)
14. Prayer to Finish what I Started (2Tim 4:7-8, Jn 17:4-10)
15. Prayer of Remembrance, Loyalty, & Devotion to God (Deut 8:2-10)

16. Prayer to Preach the Word of God (Tim 4:1-5, Ja 3:1-2;8, Ja 5:19-20)
17. Prayer for Troubled Teens (Pr20:11, 2Tim 2:22, Pr 22:6)
18. Prayer for Children in Foster Care (Lk 9:47-48, Is 1:17, Ja 1:27, Ps 146:9, Pr 22:6)
19. Prayer for My Baby's Mother(s) (1Tim 5:5-8)
20. Prayer for Unresolved Issues between Family & Friends (Eph 4:26; 4:31, Ja 4:1, Ja 5:9)
21. Prayer for My Heart, Emotions & Attitude (1Chr 28:9, 1Cor 3:18, Ja 4:7-10)
22. Prayer for Non-Believers (Lk 24:25, Jn 5:37-38, Ja 7:5, Ja 5:19-20)
23. Prayers for Disciples of Christ (Lk 10:1-3, Lk 9:59-62, 2Thess 3:1-5, Lk 14:25-30)
24. Prayer for the Prostitutes (Heb 11:31, Josh 6:25, Ja 2:24-25)
25. Prayer for all Tribes, Nations & Races (Deut 1:10-18, 1Tim 2:1-4, Col 1:9,10, Is 55:7, Ps 59:1; 67:3)
26. Prayer to Lead by Example (1Tim 4:12-16)
27. Prayer for the Mentally Ill (Mk 9:25, Is 35L6)
28. Prayer for the Poor (Lk 6:20-22, Ja 2:1, Ja 2:5-6, ja 2:15; 2:8-9)
29. Prayer for Spiritual Maturity (Heb 5:12-14)
30. Prayer for those who Spitefully Use Me (Mt 5:44-48)

31. Prayer for Instruction (2Tim 3:15-17)
32. Prayer for the Theif (Pr 6:30; 29:24, Jn 12:6, Eph 4:28)
33. Prayer for Prosperity (1Cor 16:2, 3Jn 2, Josh 1:8, 2Chr 26:5, Is 53:10)
34. Prayer for the Drug Addict
35. Prayer for the Doctors (Mt 19:13-15, Pr 22:6)
36. Prayer for the Drug Dealers (2Cor 2:11, Ez 14:6, Zec 1;4, Gal 5:19-20)
37. Prayer for the Work of My Hands (Ecc 9:10, Ja 2:20-21)
38. Prayer for My Marriage (Ecc 9:9)
39. Prayer for Wisdom (Ecc 9:16-18, Pr 29:3, Pr 4:5-9)
40. Prayer to do the Will of God in Christ Jesus (1Thess 5:12-23, Ja 4:15)
41. Prayer for Sanctification in My Life (1Thess 5:24, Ja 4:17)
42. Prayer to Conquer all My Troubles (Acts 7:10, Rom 8:35-37)
43. Prayer for Power to face Opposition (Acts 4:29-31, Ps 91:13)
44. Prayer for the Fruit of the Spirit (Gal 5:22-23, Mt 7:17, Jn 15:8, Eph 5:9)
45. Prayer Against Procrastination (Pr 6:6-11, Pr 13:4, Pr 19:15, Ja 2:17)
46. Prayer for a New Perspective (Ro 12:12, Neh 4:6, Col 3:2)

47. Prayer for My Thoughts (2Cor 10:5, 1Cor 13:11, 1Chr 28:9, Ps 19:59, Heb 10:16, Phil 2:13)
48. Prayer for My Child in School (Mt 19:13-15, Pr 22:6)
49. Prayer for Black Women (Ez 16:10-14)
50. Prayer for the Gospel Singer (Ez 33:30-33)
51. Prayer to Seek God Daily (1Chr 28:9, Mt 7:7, 2Chr 15:2, Ps 25:10, Pr 7:23)
52. Prayer for Courage (1Chr 28:20, 2Chr 15:7)
53. Prayer for those Who Intend to Harm Me (Gen 50:20, 2Tim 4:14-18)
54. Prayer to be Content on Everything (Heb 13:5, 1Tim 6:6-10, Phil 4:11)
55. Prayer for the Fruit of Righteousness (2Cor 9:10, Ja 3:17-18, Heb 12:11)
56. Prayer for Forgiveness of My Sins (Ps 103:3, Eph 1:7, Acts 13:38)
57. Prayer for My Mother (Jn 19:27, Ex 20:12, Mt 10:37, Job 1:21, Mk 3:35)
58. Prayer for My Father (Pr 17:6, Gen 31:5, Ps 27:100, Mt 10:37)
59. Prayer for Happiness in My Life (2Cor 12:9, 2Tim 2:1, 2Pet 3:8-10)
60. Prayer for God's Grace in My Life (Rom 14:22, Pr 16:20, Pr 2:13)
61. Prayer for My Friends & Friends to Come (Ja 2:23, Pr 18:24; 17:17; 18:24)
62. Prayer for My Employer (Mt 20:1-6, Col 4:1)

63. Prayer for the Ghetto's (Ps 69:33; 74:21; 41:17)
64. Prayer for the Prisoner's (Ps 69:33, Mt 25:36, Acts 5:19; 16:26, 2Tim 2)
65. Prayer for Discernment (Heb 5:14, Pr 2:1-6; 2:11-12)
66. Prayer for My Daughter (1Pet 3:5-6, Acts 2:17)
67. Prayer for Justice (Job 34:12, Ps 37:28-29, Lk 18:7-8)
68. Prayer for Our Elders (1Pet %:1, Ps 105:22)
69. Prayer against the Spirit of Suicide (Mt 5:21, Acts 16:27031, Rom 7:11)
70. Prayer for when I'm Suffering & Afflicted (Job 6:14; 34:28, Ps 140:12)
71. Prayer for when I'm Traveling (Ps 23:2; 23:3, Deut 28:3-6)
72. Prayer for God's Favor (Ps 5:12: 30:5, Acts 7:10)
73. Prayer for My Brother(s) (Heb 13:1-3, 1Pet 3:8, Mk 3:35
74. Prayer for My Sister(s) (Song 8:8, Mt 12:50, Mk 3:35)
75. Prayer against Curses upon Me, My Family & Generation (Gen 12:3, Neh 13:2, Lk 6:28)
76. Prayer to Overcome Limitations (Ps 78:41, Job 15:8, Pr 8:29)
77. Prayer to Overcome Pride & Arrogance (Pr 8:13, Is 13:11; 10:12, Ez 24:21)

78. Prayer for Humility (Deut 8:12, Ps 25:9; 147:6, 1Pet 5:5, Col 3:12)
79. Prayer for My Ex-Wife (Mt 5:31-32)
80. Prayer for My Neighbors (Ps 28:3, Gal 5:14, Pr 14:21)
81. Prayer for when I feel Lonely (Jn 16:32, Jn 8:29)
82. Prayer to Rebuke Jealousy & Envy (Ps 23:17, Pr 24:21)
83. Prayer for the Alcoholic (Rom 13:13, Gal 5:21, 1Thess 5:2)
84. Prayer for Patience (Lk 8:15; 21:19, 1Thess 1:3, Ja 1:4)
85. Prayer for Men & Women in the Service (2Tim 2:3; 2:4, Rome 13:12, Eph 6:11)
86. Prayer for Law Enforcement (Rom 13:1, Tit 3:1, 1Tim 1:9, Gal 3:24; 2:19)
87. Prayer for when all Hope is Lost (Acts 24:15, Heb 11:1, Ps 39:7, Zec 9:12)
88. Prayer for Self Control (1Cor 7:5; 7:9, 1Tim 2:15, 2Pet 1:6)
89. Prayer to always Seek the Lord (Chr 22:19, Ps 34:10, Jer 29:11-14)
90. Prayer for the Lord's Anointing (2Cor 1:21, Lk 4:18, Ps 20:6, 2Sam 22:51)
91. Prayer to Rebuke the Spirit of Lust (Pr 6:25, Gal 5:16, 1Jn 2:16, Ro 1:24-25)
92. Prayer for the Right Answer (Pr 15:23; 24:26, Is 65:24 Ps 61:15)

93. Prayer to Follow Jesus (Mt 4:19; 18:22; 10:38, Mk 8:34)
94. Prayer to Rest & Be Still (Ps 16:9, Rev 14:13, 2Thess 1:7, Mk 4:39)
95. Prayer for the LBGT Community (1Cor 6:9-11, Rom 1:7)
96. Prayer for Confidence (Heb 10:35, 2Thess 3:4, Ps 118:8, Pr 3:26)
97. Prayer to Resist the devil (1Pet 5:8-9, Ja 4:7)
98. Prayer for My Loved Ones Who Have Passed Away (Rom 14:9, Pr 18:21, He 2:9)
99. Prayer for Pastors, Preachers & Ministers of God (

Intro

Prayer to Mentor

(Mt 4:18-19)

In my personal opinion and from my life's experiences, having a mentor is a valuable asset one can have. Being a mentor is similar to being a shepherd because you are instructing, guiding and leading an individual in the direction of their full potential. A mentor listens and sometimes instructs. Having mentors in our churches and communities are vital. Mentors in our schools and our homes are important in the spiritual growth and development of our youth.

When you pray to mentor you're praying that you also carry yourself with honor, respect, and integrity that you are leading by example and that your actions speak louder than words. You are praying for the wisdom, knowledge and understanding to carry out this responsibility entrusted upon you.

If you were called to be a mentor, then this is a divine appointment given to you especially as a gift from God. So please treat it as a gift. It's important to examine ourselves daily as we go through life. Exercise the fruits of the spirits' muscles because you will most definitely need to have a little joy, peace, patience, kindness, goodness, humility, self-control, gentleness, and most important of them all

is love. Although you're a mentor, always remember that you're never too old or too young to learn something new about yourself or discover your purpose in life. You are never too old to be a mentor or mentee.

As you mentor, pray with your mentee when faced with life changing situations, important decisions or problems, because at the end of the day, God is in control and his grace is sufficient enourh for us in everything we face in life.

May God Bless you as you grow in your mentoring ministry, and if you are a mentee, then may God bless you in your relationship.

Prayer

To Mentor

Matthew 4:18-19

Heavenly Father,

I come to you in the name of Jesus to thank you for the opportunity and responsibility you have given me to mentor. Thank you for entrusting me with such a position Lord. I ask that you give me the wisdom, knowledge and understanding to be a positive influence in the lives of the people I mentor. Create in me the qualities to lead him or her into a productive, healthy, successful lifestyle that honors you Lord. Father give me the strength, and allow me the time to be there for my mentee's whenever or however I'm called upon.to serve.

May my life, words and actions be in accordance with Your will Father God in which you called me to be a mentor in my community. I pray that I may also learn and grow in wisdom, knowledge and understanding in this calling upon my life Lord.

I lift up the people you have put in my life, their family, friends, neighbors and peers. I pray that they continue to grow in love and purpose in life. I pray that these relationships between Your children are always a reflection of You and Your Son Jesus Christ.

Intro

Prayer for Inspiration

(Lk 12:2)

Whether you admit it or believe it or not, we are all inspired by something or someone. Even a tragedy can inspire us to want to live a healthier life and make better decisions. To take that chance on a business venture, or go and get that job you don't feel qualified to take on. A bad break up or divorce can inspire us to be a better partner through counseling and the reading and doing of God's Word. Inspiration can lead us to focus more on the Lord and our talent's gifts and abilities. A teacher can inspire us to follow our dreams or pastor can inspire us to serve our communities in a special way. The Bible can inspire us to seek God's will, plan, and purpose for our lives. Incarceration can inspire to get out get an education, write a book, or become an advocate for change.

My point is that inspiration is flowing through us and all around us both subtly and blatantly. The question you have to ask yourself is "what inspires me?" As you pray, be thankful for this inspiration even if you don't recognize it right away. God will surely bring it to your attention and inspire you to do something, say something or be something. Ask God to continue sending you inspirational people and moments because we need this inspiration to fulfill our purpose in life. God's love inspires us. That's why He sent His Son Jesus to die on the Cross for our sins because with every evil spirit drove out, everyone He healed, or spoke to was an inspiration to us.

We should be inspired as Christians to walk in love like our savior Jesus did. We should be inspired to forgive others because God forgives us through the blood of His Son Jesus Christ. We should be inspired to give freely because Jesus freely gave His life for us.

Allow inspiration to work in your life and discover God's will for your life.

Prayer

For Inspiration

Lk 12:12

Heavenly Father,

I thank You for all the people I know, the places I've seen and the life You have given me. Thank you for the inspiration you have placed all around me in your creation Father God. Thank you for the inspiration I have to grow and become a better person each and every day. Thank you for the inspiration that comes in its purest form to lead me

INTRO

Prayer for My Talents, Gifts & Abilities

(Mt 25:14-29, 1Cor 12)

Although love should be our goal in life, God has blessed each and every one of us with various talents, gifts, and abilities. It's a spiritual gift that we should always be thankful for. It's what gives our lives meaning and substance. You can use these spiritual gifts at home, in the community, at work, in school, on the bus, or wherever you are.

Someone may be more spiritually gifted than others, but that doesn't even matter because the Bible tells us in 1 Corinthians 12:4 that all our spiritual gifts are from the same spirit. It also goes on to tell us that there are different ways to serve, but we serve the same Lord. We serve the church, our cities, communities, states and neighborhoods in everything that we do whether you know it or not. We are using our talents, gifts, and abilities everywhere we go and in everything we do.

It's easy to get caught up in using our spiritual gifts for purposes that are outside of God's will, especially if it will offer us a little bit of extra comfort, money and security. For example someone gifted in math could be tempted to take advantage of and abuse the church funds or embezzle the company they work for. But since love should be our ultimate guide in life, then our love wouldn't allow us to hurt the church or jeopardize our place of business.

So, have you discovered your own talents, gifts and abilities yet? Is it the ability to speak or write with knowledge? Are you gifted in having faith and sharing that faith? Maybe you're a doctor who has the gift to heal and perform miraculous healings through surgery and other procedures. Perhaps you have the gift of intuition and prophecy. Can you sing and lift your voice to the Lord? Are you a good teacher? Do you speak more than one language? Do you know sign language? Are you good at building things and designing buildings? So don't be like the unfaithful servant who hid his talents in the ground until his master came back home..

Prayer

For my Talents, Gifts & Abilities

(Mt 25:14-29 1Cor 12:4-7)

Heavenly Father,

I thank you so much for my talents, gifts and abilities. It is such a blessing to be so talented and gifted according to the aility you gave me. Lord, I pray that I don't take my talents, gifts, and abilities for granted, and that I use them for your purpose and will for my life. I pray that I don't use and abuse my talents, gifts or abilities for evil, or lead people astray. I understand that if I am faithful with my talents, gifts, and abilities, they will be multiplied. In the name of Jesus I pray that I remain faithful in any and every talent, gift and ability you have entrusted me with.

Amen

Intro

Prayer for Peace

(Heb 12:14, 2Tim 2:22, Ps 34:14, Mt 10:13; 10:34, Ro 8:6)

The word peace was mentioned more than 55 times throughout the Holy Bible. Jesus tells us in John 14:27 that He leaves us with peace and He gives us peace. However, Jesus tells us that He doesn't give us a peace that the world gives us. It's a different kind of peace that we're praying for here. It's a different kind of peace that we are seeking. The kind of peace that Jesus gives us is the peace that banishes fear and dread from our hearts. Its' the kind of peace that surpasses all understanding and it lets us know that Jesus is in control of all our circumstances. The Jewish people say "Shalom" which means peace in Hebrew.

The Bible tells us that we are to pursue peace with all people and do our best to live right and have faith and love. We are to do this together with others who trust in the Lord with pure hearts. In doing so, we avoid foolish arguments that escalate.

We must be kind and patient with each other's shortcomings and faults. We should gently teach those who don't agree with us. God has a way of changing people's hearts to accept what is noble, just and true.

The Word tells us in Romans 8:6 that to have a carnal mind is to be an enemy of God and leads to death. But to be spiritually minded is life and peace. Peace is being in harmony within yourself and having a tranquil mind as a result of submitting to God. If you want to be blessed, then be a peacemaker because peacemakers shall be called sons of God. (Matthew 5:9)

As you pray for peace, remember to pray for peace in our homes, in our states, cities, communities, churches and schools. Pray for world peace. Pray to be a peacemaker. Peace be with you.

Prayer

For Peace

(Jn 14:27))

Heavenly Father,

I lift my heart to you right not to thank you for the peace that surpasses all understanding. Thank you for the peace that our Lord and Savior Jesus Christ left us when he came into this world. Jehovah God, I ask you to step into my situation, my life, and my heart right now and give me peace. Give my family, friends, loved ones and communities' peace Father God. Let not my heart be troubled, neither let it b afraid, because of my past, present, or future circumstances. I pray that you remove all fear and dread from my heart through your Son Jesus Christ I pray.

Amen.

Intro

Prayer to Be of Service

(Ps 110:3, Jn 13:4, Lk 22:19)

Being of service is the perfect example of our faith in God and Christ. Being of service in our homes, cites, communities, churches, schools and places of business. Being of service to our fellow man, woman, or by helping those less fortunate than us, or sharing an encouraging word.

There are many ways to be of service in case you need a brief refresher course on the subject. You can serve by volunteering at your local soup kitchen, feeding the homeless, mentoring like we prayed for previously. You can volunteer at your local senior citizen homes, or to assist the youth and adults with learning disabilities, or children with special needs. Even carrying the groceries to the car for a single mother is an act of service. For the men, we can be of service by being a gentleman to the women in our communities by opening a door for them.

In the Bible, Jesus showed the ultimate act of service and taught us a very valuable lesson on service. In Luke 22:26 He teaches us that the ones with the most authority among you should act as if he is the least important and the one who leads should be like one who serves. He goes on to teach us in the very next verse that the one serving at the dinner table is more important. It's obvious that the one serving the dinner at the table is more important because without them serving then they wouldn't eat or would have to prepare their own food. When Jesus washed His disciple's feet, he did this as an example for us to serve each other just as He served us. This is the most humble and noble act of love is being of service to one another.

As you pray to be of service, whose feet will you begin washing?

Prayer

To Be of Service

(Ps. 110:3, John 13:14, Lk 22:19)

Dear Lord,

I lift my prayers to You in the name of Your Son Jesus Christ. I thank You for the humble example that Jesus set when He washed the feet of His disciple Simon Peter. I understand that this was the ultimate act of love by being of service to one another. Father God, I pray that You use me to be of service to the community and people You put in my path. I pray that I serve others cheerfully and compassionately, without showing partiality or passing judgment. I thank You for the blessings and favor that come along with being of service. In the name of Jesus I pray these prayers and petitions.

Amen.

INTRO

Prayer for our Designers, Builders & Body of the Church.

(Ex 36:1, Ezra 1:5, 1Cor 3:10)

I'm sure that we've all been to beautiful churches all around the world with beautiful architecture, stained glass windows, and art that tells the history of the Church and Body of Christ. Pictures of Jesus, the Last Supper, Holy Angels, the Virgin Mary and other Biblical Characters for worshipers to get spiritual inspiration from. To make worshipers feel welcome in the house of the Lord as we fellowship together.

There were gifted artisans in biblical times (Ex 36:1) that the Lord blessed with wisdom and understanding to know how to do all manners of work for the service of the sanctuary. These artisans designed the churches and sanctuaries upon God's demand. This particular work called for a very careful and detailed artistic work. The same applies to today's artisans and architects. It takes skill to design and build a church from the inside out. It is the house of the Lord, and not commercial property.

Our churches are where countless lives are being saved, broken hearts are mended, communities are united, and souls are gathered as one in the presence of God. Our churches are where we come together to worship, praise, and hear the word of God; taught to us by preachers, pastors, ministers, and musicians where we fellowship in the body of Christ.

As we pray for our designers, builders and body of the Church and respect the House of the Lord that is within each and every one of us as we congregate in our communities, we are all one Body of Christ which makes up the House of the Lord.

Prayer

For our Designers, Builders & Body of the Church.

(Ex 36:1, Ezra 1:5, 1Cor 3:10)

Heavenly Father,

I thank You for the Church in which I belong. I thank You for all that Churches, Temples, and Sanctuaries all around the world. Thank You for the wisdom and understanding of every gifted architect who had a vision to make our Churches beautiful to represent the House of the Lord. I pray that You continue to bless the ones You have chosen to visualize, plan, design, and build Your Churches from the inside out. I pray that each sanctuary is a reflection of Your love, where believers and unbelievers feel loved and welcome together as we fellowship in the Body of Christ. In the name of Jesus I pray this prayer.

Amen

INTRO

Prayer for My Enemies

(Rom 12:17-21, Lk 6:27, Ps 18:3, 23:5, 119:98)

Believe it or not, all of us have an enemy. There is one enemy tha we all share, and that is satan. The one enemy we all have tries to cause us many problems, and grief in our home life, family, marriages, friendships, work, our churches, neighborhoods and communities.

Our greatest weapon against the enemy isn't fighting with guns, knives, or any kind of violence. That's what the enemy wants us to do is kill and destroy us with wars and violence among eachother. The word of God says in Ephesians 6 that we must wear the full armor of God so that we can fight against the devils clever tricks. It goes on to say that our fight isn't against the people on earth, but our fight is against the principalities, against powers, the rulers of darkness of this age. And against spiritual hosts of wickedness in the heavenly places. In other words, we are in the middle of spiritual warfare. Demonic beings work through people we least expect. Sometimes the people closest to us. That's why its important to stay prayed up as spiritual leaders in our homes and communities.

Finally, the Word tells us to love our enemies. At times the people we love curse us or treat us unfairly and hate on us for one reason or another. The Bible tells us to love them and do good to them; bless those who curse us, and pray for the people who use us and take advantage of us (Lk 6:27-28).

As we follow these instructions given to us in the Word, the Lord is already preparing to save us from our enemies (Ps 23:5). The Lord has made us wiser than our enemies (Ps 119:98). As we pray for our enemies, love them and do good to them, remember that God has already delivered us from evil by the blood of Jesus Christ.

PRAYER

For My Enemies

(Rom 12:17-21, Luke 6:27)

Dear Heavenly Father,

In Your Word, You tell me to live peaceably with all men, not to avenge myself, and give place to wrath, because vengeance is Yours Father God, and You will repay. You also told me to love my enemies and do good to those who hate me. Lord God, this is a hard thing for me to do. But I pray that you give me the wisdom, knowledge, understanding, and strength to apply these principles in my everyday life. I pray that I never make any enemies or do anything to cause hatred from anyone I encounter. If I have made any enemies, I pray that You heal whatever happened between us and that we forgive one another of any wrong doings. I pray that you replace any hatred towards me with love, peace, patience, kindness, gentleness and self-control. I also pray for my enemies, their families, friends, and loved ones. I now lift this prayer and petition to You Father God, in the name of Jesus I pray.

Amen.

Prayer for the Writer

(Rev 1:19, Ps 45:1, Jn 5:46-47, Ex 24:12)

Thank God for the gifted writers from the past and present. Where would we be had God not prompted Moses to write the 10 commandments and communicate Gods laws with us. What about the writers who God spoke with in the teachings of the Bible? Through the Holy Spirit, God prompted countless men and women to write Hymns and spiritual self-help books throughout the decades.

The Lord has given many of us the gift to write and share our testimonies and minister through our writing. Just go to the library, read our history books, or look online. People are doing more writing than they are talking. Sharing our thoughts, views, opinions and experiences with the world. We are doing so much writing that we need publishers and editors to make sure we get credit for our writing and make sure we aren't plagiarized.

What about the writers of the Bible? Who was their publisher? Who did their editing and copyrights? Did they have a publicist and PR? Absolutely! It was the Lord! It was God and the Holy Spirit. In Revelations 1:19, Christ commands us to "write the things which you have seen, and which are, and the things which will take place after this". I often read the Bible in present tense because that's how the Lord instructs us is through the Bible, which is the living Word of God. It makes perfect sense that we should write what we've seen, and the things which are, and the things that will take place after this. We are living in prophetic times, so why not keep a written record of our personal journeys, thoughts and contributions?

As we pray for the writers, I would advise you to also use your writing abilities to blog or keep a journal of you daily life experiences. Take the time to write that book you've always wanted to write. Write your own prayers and letters to God, and keep a record of answered and unanswered prayers. Write about your trials and tribulations, and how the Lord has brought you through them. Write about the things you have seen, the things which are, and things as they come.

PRAYER

For the Writer

(Rev 1:19, Ps 45:1, Jn 5:46-47, Ex 24:12)

Heavenly Father,

I thank you for blessing my mind and giving me the ability to express myself in writing. I pray that I will use my writing to inspire, motivate, enlighten, and educate my readers. I pray that in all I write Father God, that you speak through me and allow my words to flow freely with wisdom, knowledge and understanding. Lord, I pray that I never allow the enemy to compromise my integrity and truth in my writing, and that my words only reflect the fruits of the spirit. I pray this prayer in the name of Jesus.

Amen

INTRO

For the Gospel Singer

(Ez 33:30-33, 2Sam 22:50, Ps 33:3)

Yes, our gospel singers need our prayers too! What joy it brings to our hearts and souls to hear the choir sing before the pastors and preachers give us the Word of God. The sounds resonate in our hearts and stir up our souls with the Holy Spirit as we lift our voices to worship and praise the Lord God and our Savior Jesus Christ.

In Ezekiel 33:30-33, the Lord tells the Prophet Ezekiel that he has a good voice, but he is nothing to the exiles in Babylon, but a singer singing love songs and one who plays the instrument well. That the exiles only listen to his words, but will not do what the prophet says. The people would get up and sing along with him, clap their hands, and stomp their feet; but it was only for entertainment.

Today, we get so caught up in the entertainment aspect of gospel music that we often miss the message and word of the songs. There are praise songs, and songs of worship. But there are also songs that prophecy and give testimony. There are songs that minister to us beautifully and artistically. David sings songs of thanks and worship. Not to mention he shares the testimony of his life through his music, and his life is literally an open book. In the book of 2 Samuel 22:50 you will find his music. Whenever God would do a new and wonderful thing for the people, they would write a new song about it (Ps 33:3). Wisdom, knowledge and understanding are shared in gospel music there are Christian rappers emerging from all over the country from various backgrounds, cultures, and communities. So many people are sharing their story and their testimonies; crying out to God and ministering about His grace and mercy.

As we pray for our Gospel singers, I challenge you the next time you go to church or a Gospel music concert, or play a Gospel CD in your car, or listen to Gospel radio on Pandora; that you listen intently to the message behind the lyrics for wisdom, knowledge, understanding, discernment, prophecy, and encouragement, which goes without saying. Lift your voice to the Lord and sing a new song, but also open your hearts and ears to the Word of God.

PRAYER

For the Gospel Singer

(Ez 33:30-33, 2 Sam 22:50, Ps 33:3)

Heavenly Father,

Oh Lord, how I thank you for this amazing gift to lift my voice to you. I thank you for all of the Gospel singers and Christian rappers all over the world. I pray for those who aspire to lift their voices to sing praises and to minister to believers and non-believers alike. I thank you for all the Gospel singers and rappers who have the gift to share their testimonies through musical genius. I pray that we continue to lift our voices and that you give us all new songs to sing that will minister and glorify your name and our personal Lord and Savior Jesus Christ. I pray that our voices aren't lifted only to entertain people, but to worship and praise You Lord. I pray that listeners not only hear our words, but that they penetrate their hearts and ignite the Holy Spirit within us. Thank you Father God for all of the songs you give your people to sing in the name of Jesus I pray this prayer.

Amen.

INTRO

Prayer for Our Lawyers

(Lk 11:46, Ro 7:14, Ps 19:7)

According to the NKJV Study Bible; the Greek term for law means an inward principle of action, either good or evil operating with the regularity of law. According to the Webster's dictionary, law is a ruse established by authority, society, or custom. A profession relating to such rules. A lawyer is a professional who practices law.

In Luke 11:46, Jesus reproached the experts in law because they made strict rules that are very hard for people to obey and try to force others to obey these rules when they themselves don't even try to follow those very same rules. This was a bold teaching that applies to today as well. Society is burdened with enough laws to fill the white house from top to bottom. There are so many new laws coming up each day that it's hard to keep up with them.

That's why it's important to pray for our lawyers and law makers because they not only place heavy burdens on us spoken of in the Bible, but they are heavily burdened themselves to uphold and defend these laws in the interest of justice. It's much easier if we would just do away with all the laws of the world and replace them with the original law which is the law of the Lord written in Ps 19:7-8, the Word says that the Law of the Lord is perfect, converting the soul. The testimony of the Lord is sure, making wise the simple; and the Statutes of the Lord are right, rejoicing the heart. The Commandment of the Lord is pure, enlightening to the eyes.

As we pray for the Lawyers & Law Makers, let's keep it simple and abide by the Law of the Lord, which is to love God with all our hearts, and love our neighbors as we love ourselves. In doing so, that will keep us out of court. This is the ultimate crime prevention and civil settlement strategy because if we love God and our neighbors, then we wouldn't do anything to break the Spiritual Laws of or the world's law. At the end of the day, we are all sinners justified by the grace of God.

PRAYER

For Our Lawyers

(Lk 11:26, Rom 7:14, Ps 19:7)

Dear Heavenly Father,

I lift up all of our lawyers across the world right now in the name of Jesus. I understand their position is to know the laws, defend, the law, and uphold the law. However, no one is perfect, not even a lawyer, for we are all sinners and fall short of the glory. I pray that our lawyers, district attorneys, and paralegals serve our courthouses with wisdom, knowledge, understanding, and compassion. I pray that the lawyers and District Attorneys serve our courthouses with dignity, honor and respect for spiritual laws and Biblical knowledge in all aspects of the criminal and civil justice system. I pray that the Lawyers and DA's don't put heavy sentences on those arrested for petty crimes and substance abuse, and that those convicted can get the help they need to live productive, successful lives according to your will in the name of Jesus I pray.

Amen.

INTRO

Prayer for the Judges

(Rom 13:4-5, Deut 1:16-18)

I know you've heard the famous lyrics by Tupac Shakur "Only God Can Judge Me." That saying has been used countless times in our communities no matter what part of the country you live in. It's true that God is the true judge, however, He does appoint rulers and judges to help us. They have the power to punish us, and they will according to Romans 13:4. They are God's servants to punish those of us who do wrong. The Bible tells us in Romans 13:5 that we must obey the government, not just because we might be punished, but because we know it's the right thing to do.

I've had my fair share of listening to the lyrics of "Only God Can Judge Me." But now that I'm wiser in the Word of God; it's not the judgment of our appointed judges that Tupac was condemning, but the judgment that people pass on each other. In Romans 2, the Word says that man is inexcusable for passing judgment on each other, and that in whatever we judge one another, we are condemning ourselves because we who pass judgment, practice the same things in which we are judging. The Word goes on to say, "But we know the judgment of God is according to truth against those who practice such things." The Lord is the only one who has the right to judge us because of the richness of His goodness, forbearance and longsuffering, not knowing that the goodness of God leads us to repentance.

As we pray for our judges, let us also repent of our sins and ask for God's forgiveness as we strive for perfection in the image and likeness of Christ Jesus. Let us not refuse to change and avoid making our punishments greater and greater, because of our sins. Let us live daily for God's glory and honor. And when we do feel the need to judge, then do so righteously through prayer and repentance for our brothers and sisters. Remember, only God can judge.

PRAYER

For the Judges

(Rom 13:4-5, Deut 1:16-18)

Heavenly Father,

I know that you are the true God of justice for your creation. I thank You for mercy and grace through Your Son Jesus Christ. Thank You for the grace that allows me to learn from my mistakes and come into repentance. I thank You for all the governing authorities and judges that withhold the laws. I pray that they will continue to judge and uphold the law with wisdom, mercy, integrity, and love. Lord, I know that You judge people through human authorities here to set us straight on the path back to repentance and redemption from our wrongs. I repent right now in the name of Jesus for any sin I have committed in my mind, body, and spirit. I pray that you forgive me for any crimes I may have committed in the past, and for violating any of mans laws. I pray that when I'm judged, that I am judged righteously, and only punished the way You see fit for Your plan and purpose in my life. In the mighty name of Jesus I pray these prayers and petitions.

Amen.

INTRO

Prayer for Gangs & Gang Members

(Is 11:6, Is 2:4)

We are plagued with a culture of groups and organizations that bond in brother and sisterhood, fraternities, and even political parties. One group always opposes another group, as they share different beliefs, grew up on a different side of town, come from different cultures, on other factors. Many of us know at least one person (family member, friend, or associate) who belongs to some form of gang in the community.

According to the Merriam-Webster dictionary, a gang is defined as; (1): a group of persons working together, (2): a group of persons working to unlawful or antisocial ends; especially a band of antisocial adolescents. (3): a group of persons having informal and usually close social relations.

There is a history behind every gang in our communities, and people who were disadvantaged economically, politically, or racially challenged, amongst other contributing factors formed them. Some gangs formed to fight for equality, freedom, justice, equal rights, and protection for their often-close knitted communities. However, much violence has occurred, and often times more problems are created because of gang activity. The crime rate went up, people lost their lives, and families have been broken up and destroyed because of gang activity.

As we pray for these gangs, gang members, and the leaders, let us refer to the Bible as we pray for unity and peace. In Is 11:6, a perfect picture of this unity and peace is a painted where the wolf dwells with the lamb; the leopard lies down with the young goat, and the calf and the young lion and the fatling are together. Can you imagine wolves dwelling with lambs, and leopards lying down with goats? The final verse in Is 6:6, says that a little child shall lead them. Sometimes, that is what it takes is for us to witness the innocence of a child to change and lead us. Only prayer and the power of God can give us a new nature of peace, harmony and unity amongst each other. No matter what gang you are from, no what tribe or reputation you carry around; God can and will deliver us from evil. Like they used to say on the 92.3 The Beat " stop the violence, increase the peace."

PRAYER

For Gangs & Gang members

(Is 11:6, Is 2:4)

Heavenly Father,

I come to You right now in the authority of Jesus Christ to lift up our brothers, sisters, and children in our communities who belong to or are affiliated with gangs. I may or may not understand the gang culture Lord, but I pray for miraculous healing and peace in our neighborhoods. I pray that the wolves may live at peace with the lambs, and leopards will lie down with goats, and that calves, lions, and bulls will all live together in peace and harmony. I pray that the gang violence will cease in our country, and that you change the hearts, minds, direction and leadership of gangs that will build our communities and protect them instead of destroying them. I pray that all of the gang members will come to an understanding of the Love of Christ, and fight for their salvation. I pray that we become great leaders in our homes, jails, and institutions across the country. Thank You Father God for answering my prayers and petitions in the name of Jesus I pray.

Amen.

In Biblical terms, a prostitute was known as a "harlot." According to the NKJV Study Bible, a harlot is the word for a common prostitute. As we speak, there is a battle going on not only to curb prostitution, but to help the countless girls and women who have been sexually exploited throughout our communities. There are wraparound services offered by juvenile halls, placement in group homes, gang intervention programs, educational opportunities, job training and even family reunification services.

Prostitution is beyond being a moral and ethical issue in our society. From a spiritual standpoint, it's an issue that must be faced head on through prayer. There is a story in the Bible about a Canaanite prostitute named Rahab. Her story is one of the most inspiring stories in the Bible that should be shared more often. She lived with her father, mother, brothers, and all that she had. Why she was a prostitute could be debated, and it's probably one of the many reasons women are sexually exploited today; poverty, sexual, physical, and mental abuse, impoverished families, abandonment, neglect, and broken homes. Even under those possible circumstances, Rehabs' faith in God led her to hide and care for the 2 Israelite spies who were in enemy territory. Rahab lied to the men who were looking for these 2 spies who came to view the land that God was preparing the Israelites to occupy. Rahab already had a hint of faith in the Lord, and all she really needed was a mustard seed of it. But she knew that God was sovereign over the heavens and earth. As a result of Rahab hiding the Israelite spies, her and her family were saved from destruction when the Israelites took over the Land of Jericho.

As we pray for the prostitutes, let us call Rahab to memory as she was a hero because of her faith. We have a moral and spiritual duty to love, honor and nurture our women and not exploit them. We have a spiritual obligation to pray for their faith that the Lord God of the Heavens and Earth will lead them, guide them, protect them, and usher them and their families safely into the body of Christ.

PRAYER

For The Prostitutes

(Heb 11:31, Josh 6:2:24-25)

Heavenly Father,

I understand that harlots like Rahab are very special women in their own way, however they came to be prostitutes Lord, I pray that you heal them of their past and present pains, hurt, affliction, and any form of sexual, physical, mental, and emotional abuse they may have suffered. I pray for their well-being and the well-being of their children as well Father God. I pray that you remove them from the people and environments that are leading the Children of God astray, and that you bring them all back into your tender loving care and mercy. I pray that You open new windows of opportunities and blessings to serve the Church, and help other children, men, and women in their communities. Lead Your Children back into Your loving arms and forgive us all of our sins. In the name of Jesus I send these prayers and petitions to You.

Amen.

INTRO

Prayer For All Tribes, Nations, & Races

(Deut 1:10-18, Gen 15:5; 22:17, Ps 147:4)

Have you ever in the middle of the night just took a moment to look at the zillions of stars in the sky? Have you ever tried to count those stars? Have you ever looked through a telescope at the 88 official constellations in the night sky? This brings us to Isaiah 40:26; " Lift up your eyes on high, and see who has created these things, who brings out their host by number; He calls them by name by the greatness of His might and the strength of His power. Not one is missing."

When it comes to tribes, nations, and races, the Lord has multiplied us and here we are today, as the stars of heaven in multitude. In the Bible, Deuteronomy 1:11; Moses prayed that the God of our fathers make the Israelites a thousand times more numerous that we are, and bless them as the Lord has promised them. There are 196 nations in the world. However, there are only 5 races which totals 7.125 billion people in the world and over 750 known tribes of people in America. The history of man goes back so far, no one really knows to start.

But our faith tells us in the Word of God, that the first man was Adam.

  As we pray for all tribes, nations & races, and call to recognition the many cultures, beliefs, differences and languages; let our prayers be the bridge to get us across our cross-cultural gaps, and strive to love one another as we love ourselves regardless of our skin color, cultural, or national background. The Lord has multiplied us for a reason, and it is not to continue to live divided amongst each other. We're praying for the breaking down of barriers, open our boarders, and tear down walls of division, pride, separatism and prejudice towards one another as a people. Like the legendary words, of an even more legendary man says; "We shall overcome some day."

PRAYER

For All Tribes, Naions & Races

(Deut 1:10-18, Gen 15:5; 22:17, Ps 147:4)

Heavenly Father,

I humbly come to You right now in word, thought, truth, and prayer to thank you for keeping your promises, and establishing a covenant with our fathers Abraham, Isaac, and Jacob to possess the land. Thank you for leading us out of Egypt into the Promised Land You swore to our fathers. Thank you Father God for multiplying every tribe and nation as the stars of heaven in multitude. Although we have cultural differences, beliefs, languages, and differences, we are all from the family of God. I pray that you stand in the middle of our cultural gaps and be our bridge to get us across to each other like you always have. Lord, I pray that you break down barriers, open our borders, and tear down walls of division, pride, separation, and prejudice towards each other as a people. In the name and blood of our savior Jesus Christ I humbly pray.

Amen.

INTRO

Prayer of Rememberance, Loyalty, & Devotion

(Deut 8:2-10, Ps 119:38, 1Ki 8:61)

Do you ever think back to a time in your life when something occurred that was or could have been so tragic, that it had to be an act of God that got you through? Has there ever been a time when you were faced with such a defining moment in your life that would forever change the course of the future you thought you had planned? Or have you ever been in trouble and cried out to God, promising that if He got you through your trouble, you would change your life around? Perhaps you asked God to help save a troubled marriage or save your child's life.

Time and time again, the Lord has come through for us and answered many of our prayers. Often times we don't even acknowledge the smallest to biggest miracles God does in our lives on a daily basis. For instance, it's a miracle that many of us are even still breathing, walking or talking. If you are reading this introduction to Prayer of Rememberance, Loyalty & Devotion to God right now, you are a miracle, and you are blessed and highly favored. Im not saying that the people who aren't reading this right now aren't blessed and highly favored, but you certainly are.

The Lord teaches us to rely on Him during our journey through life. There are tests that come along the way to humble us like the Lord did Israel during their journey through the wilderness. Eventually, the Lord will know whats in our hearts as we cry out to Him through these testings. How could we not be loyal to the God who created us and answers our prayers? How could we not devote our lives to the Son of God who died on the cross for our sins? How could we not remember how far the Lord has brought us through the wilderness?

As we pray for Rememberance, Loyalty, & Devotion to God, let us also wake up every morning in thanksgiving and praise as we go on about our days.